BayAreaStyle

Houses of the San Francisco Bay Region

BayAreaStyle

Houses of the San Francisco Bay Region

Photographs by Alan Weintraub

Text by David Weingarten

RIZZOLI
NEW YORK

First published in the United States of America in 2004 by
RIZZOLI INTERNATIONAL PUBLICATIONS, INC.
300 Park Avenue South, New York, NY 10010
www.rizzoliusa.com

ISBN: 0-8478-2640-6
LCCN: 2004092989

Designed by Zand Gee Design

Printed and bound in China

2004 2005 2006 2007 2008 / 10 9 8 7 6 5 4 3 2 1

Cover: Partington Point House, 1996

Back Cover: Teviot Springs Vineyard, 1991

Overleaf: Pence House, 1962

Contents page, left to right:
Hume Cloister 1928, Kellog House 1948,
Bulwinkleland 1986, Polk-Williams House 1892

Photography credits:

Page 9: Wyntoon, photographs from the Hans U.
Gerson and William G. Merchant Collection,
Environmental Design Archives, University of
California, Berkeley © UC Regents.

Page 11: Gregory Farmhouse, photographs by
Rodger Sturtevant. From the William W. Wurster/
WBE Collection, Environmental Design Archives,
University of California, Berkeley © UC Regents.

Page 13: Charles Moore Orinda House, all
reproduction rights reserved by the Morley Baer
Photography Trust © 2004.

Page 14: Bernard Maybeck, portrait, photograph
from the Bernard Maybeck Collection,
Environmental Design Archives, University of
California, Berkeley ©UC Regents.

Page 17: MIDDLE Hester/McNally Residence,
Edward Caldwell Photography, courtesy of Arkin
Tilt; BOTTOM C House, Bruce Tomb and John
Randolph Photography, courtesy of Interim Office
Of Architecture/IOOA.

Contents

Two Bay Region Houses

Forty-five years ago, my parents arranged to swap, for two weeks, the up-to-date home Charles Moore designed for them on the Monterey Peninsula, for a house in the Berkeley Hills. I don't recall what I anticipated with this; what does an eight year old anticipate beyond his birthday and Christmas?

Yet, what I encountered was a surprise, a kind of foreign territory, and the memory of that house is strangely vivid, especially as so much else fades. That Berkeley house was so different from my own. It rose to several floors, with an attic and a basement, and stairs snaking up through the middle of it. It seemed old (though it was probably built in the 1920s), big and well-made, interesting and eccentric (though it was probably designed by no well-known architect). I remember it, also, as mysterious, like the houses in favorite books and movies; and dark, with discrete, slightly musty rooms opening one onto the next.

I must have seen my family's house — bright and new, with a straightforward open plan, all on a single level — through new eyes when we returned from Berkeley, though I made judgments about neither place. What eight year old would, beyond enthusing that both were great places to play?

That both were part of the phenomenon of Bay Region style houses, whose history then reached back to the nineteenth century, and, now, forward into the twenty-first, also did not occur to me.

My parents lived the rest of their lives in that stylish, Bay Region house, a setting so well suited to them both that is impossible to imagine their lives led elsewhere. This book is dedicated to their memory. ■

— *David Weingarten*
  Oakland, California

Chicken a la King with Ferro-Concrete Sauce

Writing in the "Skyline" column of the October 11, 1947 *New Yorker*, the then pre-eminent architectural critic Lewis Mumford praised "that native and humane form of modernism which one might call the Bay Region style, a free yet unobtrusive expression of the terrain, the climate, and the way of life on the Coast." He noted that the "style took root almost fifty years ago in Berkeley ... and by now, on the Coast, it is simply taken for granted; no one out there is foolish enough to imagine there is any other proper way of building in our time."

Unlike the academic writing of most current architectural criticism, Mumford's column is like a letter from your most perceptive and intelligent friend. It rambles slightly, veering from discussion of the absence of tall modern buildings in Manhattan since 1930, to a favorite hotel room in Washington, DC and that city's then new National Art Gallery ("the most fatuous and faulty monument that has been erected in the last twenty years"), to Henry James, to the repudiation of functionalism in architecture ("it was time that some of our architects remembered ... what a building says as well as what it does"), to holding out Bay Area architects Bernard Maybeck and William Wurster (who "took good care that their houses did not resemble factories or museums") as examples of "this national reaction against a sterile and abstract modernism."

Even by our jaded twenty-first century sensibilities, the storm following Mumford's column was surprisingly fast-moving and vigorous, as well as angry and personal. On February 11, 1948, a symposium — "What is happening to Modern Architecture?" — was convened at New York's Museum of Modern Art, and immediately documented in a MOMA Bulletin.

What occurred that no doubt cold evening in the sanctum sanctorum of modernism can only be described as an architectural mugging. While we don't have a shaky, amateur videotape, we do have the MOMA bulletin, an almost blow-by-blow transcription. Even at the space of more than half a century, it makes a simultaneously fascinating and embarrassing read.

Though arranged in express response to Mumford's endorsement of the "Bay Region style," not a single Bay Area architect or critic spoke that evening. (Of course, it is not clear that they were actually invited.) Instead, the colloquium was almost entirely given over to the International Style's most earnest, die-hard defenders, including historians, curators and critics, and architects.

Alfred Barr, MOMA Director, led off: "...the (International) Style has developed and changed and mellowed. It has even generated reactions and created opponents here and abroad. We may mention in passing the bitter hostility of Hitler and his National Socialist architects to the International Style....parallel to the German reaction has been the Soviet revival of the stylistic chaos and pomposities of the nineteenth century." Director Barr continues, in the following paragraph, "We have among us ... some old-line functionalists, some orthodox social realists and, lastly, the designers of houses, in the style which Mr. Mumford has proposed might be called the 'Bay Region Style' ... I think we might call this kind of building the International Cottage Style."

It's a wonder Barr didn't question Bernard Maybeck's German heritage; though he might have then felt compelled to mention the pre-War enthusiasms of another of that evening's participants — Philip Johnson.

Next up is Henry Russell Hitchcock, co-author with Johnson of the influential book and MOMA exhibit *The International Style*: "the Cottage Style is concerned apparently with giving a more domestic, a looser and an easier expression to domestic architecture ... that, it seems to me, is one of the difficulties about that particular new phase of expression — that its activities are centered on what is frankly not one of the important problems of the architecture of the present day."

Walter Gropius added, "Do we really want a truly universal style to be a meeting of the Oriental and Occidental (one of the attributes of the Bay Region style, according to Mumford)? Do we want to have Chicken a la king with Ferro-Concrete Sauce everywhere in our country?"

Marcel Breuer piles on, "If 'human' is considered identical with redwood all over the place, or if it is considered identical with imperfection and imprecision, I am against it; also if it is considered identical with camouflaging architecture with planting, with nature, and with romantic subsidies."

It is left to Mumford to conclude and summarize (and retreat) "I never wrote an article that was worse understood than this little attempt at reporting what was happening in the outside world. And what is the Bay Region style? Nothing but an example of a form of modern architecture which came into existence with our growth and which is so native that people, when they ask for a building, do not ask for it in any style."

When is a style not a style? When it's the Bay Region style.

Articles followed post haste. England's *Architectural Review*, in "Bay Region Domestic," boomed that "the Bay Region style is ... a parallel development to the Modern Movement." Stateside, *Architectural Record*'s "Is There a Bay Area Style?" brought predictably non-committal responses from Bay Area architects.

By 1949, the then San Francisco Museum of Art (now SFMOMA) had mounted the exhibition "Domestic Architecture of the San Francisco Bay Region," and published a catalog featuring essays by Wurster, local architects Francis McCarthy and Clarence Mayhew, *Architectural Record* writer Elizabeth Thompson, and principally, of course, Mumford.

Mumford observes that "The Bay Region architects have given form to their very informality." Yet, for the majority of his piece, Mumford, no doubt shell-shocked from the entire business, moderates his earlier claims, mends fences with the East Coast crowd, and generally minimizes the conflict. He writes, "by some unfortunate slip, I characterized the buildings that have been assembled for this exhibition as examples of the 'Bay Region Style,' and contrasted it with the restrictive and arid formulas of the so-called "International Style."

That reference conjured up the proverbial (tea-with-lemon) tempest; chiefly because its basis and its application were misunderstood ... My purposes, I would emphasize, were entirely honorable." He adds, apologetically, "in perspective, the work of this style was part of a worldwide movement in which no single country can claim preeminence."

So much for regionalism and the "proper way of building in our time." What had all the fuss been about?

In addition to the age's most solemn modernists nursing pieties bruised by a man they'd thought one of their own, this (cup-a-joe) feud revolved around a small group of houses, built over the course of fifty years, whose differences are at least as striking as their similarities; designed by a disparate group of architects, who were nonetheless fully aware of each other's work. Taken together, it is these houses with which Mumford described (and later said he hadn't meant to) the Bay Region style.

It's a very curious style indeed. The Bay Region style is confined, with the fewest exceptions, to houses and is without formal constituent parts — without the orders of classicism, the pointed arch and quatrefoil of gothic, or any of the expressionisms characteristic of modern architecture. Yet, paradoxically, many of the signal buildings of the Bay Region style employ these architectural motives.

There have been a variety of attempts to categorize the style, to list its attributes as in a field guide. Some cite its similarities to Japanese architecture, relations to the out-of-doors, and informal, unostentatious planning arrangements. Others note that Bay Region-style houses are built and finished in wood, often redwood, and assembled with attention to craft. William Wurster, writing in the 1949 San Francisco Museum of Art catalog, described the style not formally, but as according with its physical and social environments. "Take-a-chance clients, mild, even climate, no insects or bugs, a long dry season and, above and over all, the immensity of the scene — all have had their share in shaping the design. Is it small wonder to find the vitality of architecture with these as the starting point?"

Wyntoon, Siskiyou County, 1902 (burned down 1930), Phoebe and William Randolph Hearst, Bernard Maybeck. TOP View from approach. BOTTOM Hall.

After the MOMA smackdown, it was another quarter century before someone again ventured that the Bay Area possesses a singular domestic architecture. Writing in the 1976 *Bay Area Houses*, the standard work on the subject, historian David Gebhard describes qualities of buildings in the "Bay Area Tradition," "they are always houses, they are almost always small in scale, they are above all woodsy, sheathed in redwood (often inside as well as outside), they suggest a visual mode which is vernacular and anti-urban, they seem to be related to their respective place in the landscape (urban or suburban), and they are generally filled with visual and ideological contradictions." Gebhard also notes, "Ironically those buildings which most accurately reflect the Bay Area Tradition have never been the characteristic buildings of the urban environment of the Bay Area," which, he says, are often "reasonably sophisticated interpretations of national architectural styles."

For Gebhard, the Bay Area Tradition "represents an elitist view of the architecture of the region. It is closely associated with two segments in Bay Area society — the intelligentsia (would-be or otherwise) and a segment of the area's upper middle class. Bay Area Tradition architecture has never been really popular." Especially penetrating is his observation that, unlike their Southern California counterparts "Bay Area architects tend to emphasize the 'Anglo-ness' of the rural vernacular tradition upon which they draw, especially wood-board-and batten and clapboard walls, shingle roofs, long porches supported by simple, thin square wood columns, wood-framed double-hung windows..." Wurster, for example, "used the visual language of the rural vernacular to create his specifically American forms of the thirties."

The modernist architectural historian and critic Kenneth Frampton, in his 1980 *Modern Architecture*, understands Wurster's work in "the Bay Area school" in a very different way, as part of the phenomenon of Critical Regionalism, a locally inflected variant of the International Style. Within this, Frampton also includes the Mexican and Japanese architects Luis Barragan and Tadao Ando, among many others. At first, this appears an illuminating comparison. And yet, Frampton's distaste for the scenographic and sentimental, and his suspicion of vernacular influences (all fundamental parts of Wurster's approach) are so pronounced that I wonder if this isn't yet another attempt by a modernist critic to shoehorn the achievement of yet another Bay Region architect into an ill-fitting ideological pigeonhole. Wurster's modernism is hardly Frampton's.

Of course, this variety of critical appropriation is not limited to modernists. Robert Winter's 1997 *Towards a Simpler Way of Life* proffers Wurster as an example of a California Arts and Crafts architect, in line of succession from Pasadena's brothers Greene!

Progressive Eclecticism

The English Arts and Crafts Movement, on the other hand, especially the production of William Morris, had a significant impact on the Bay Region style, especially its earliest practitioners, including Willis Polk, Ernest Coxhead, and Maybeck. This English set of motives and ideas is applied to the Bay Area in Berkeley-ite Charles Keeler's 1904 *The Simple Home*. As Winter observes, Keeler's purpose with this immediately influential book, dedicated to Maybeck, lay "in identifying a truly California style of architecture for Yankees, particularly the educated ones in Berkeley." The force of Keeler's myth-making remains potent today. In the course of touring one of the houses included here, a not small, not simple, high-order architectural confection, the owner suggested it as an example of the most famous passage from Keeler's now 100-year-old manifesto — "Hillside Architecture is Landscape Gardening around a few rooms for use in case of rain."

Yet, the roots of the Bay Region style extend back beyond Charles Keeler and William Morris, back beyond John Ruskin, for that matter; back to the mid-eighteenth century and the rise in England of the Romantic era. In his 1987 *The Dilemma of Style*, the English historian J. Mordaunt Crook observes that, "During the eighteenth century romantic attitudes transformed architectural composition. Picturesque values (that is, architecture as scenery) and associationist asthetics (that is, architecture as embodied memory) broke up the canonical harmonies of classicism."

The Picturesque, from the Italian *pittoresco* — after the manner of paintings, exemplified in the landscape painting of Claude Lorrain — "so impressed the susceptibilities of early-eighteenth-century Grand Tourists that they conditioned the Englishman's way of seeing for more than one hundred years," according to Crook. With this, architecture is posited as one element among others in the composition of the natural (or, at least, natural-looking) landscape. Architecture's role in this "picture" is obtained largely through style. Crook again, "stylistic choices act as triggers to the imagination. In this way, the notion of appropriate character in architecture — the idea of a style for each mood, and a mood for each style — eventually emerged full-blown as the theory of architectural association."

More than 150 years later, this idea explicitly propels Maybeck's work. In the 1915 *Palace of Fine Arts and Lagoon*, he writes of his design for the Palace, "the process is similar to that of matching the color of ribbons. You pick up a blue ribbon, hold it alongside the sample in your hand, and at a glance you know it matches, or does not. You do the same with architecture; you examine a historic form and see whether the effect it produced on your mind matches the feeling you are trying to portray."

Warren Gregory Farmhouse,
Scotts Valley, 1928, William Wurster,
Rodger Sturtevant photographer.
TOP Courtyard view toward tower,
showing original redwood round paving.
MIDDLE Covered porch, adjacent to
living room. BOTTOM Living room.

By the first part of the nineteenth century, in England and elsewhere, the Picturesque use of architectural style for emotional purposes was no longed limited to large-scale landscape compositions. When, in *The Art Bulletin* (1950), historian C.L.V. Meeks identifies the five qualities shared by mid-nineteenth century English Picturesque buildings — roughness, movement ("rising and falling, advancing and receding"), irregularity, variety, and intricacy — he might as well be describing Bay Region style houses, through to the present day. Similarly resonant is this, also from Meeks, "I propose to call the architecture of the last century (in England) — a combination of a new form vision, the picturesque, with the limitless repertory of historic detail — "picturesque eclecticism." In identifying picturesque-ness with architectural symbolism, he adds "The Romanesque cathedral or the modern Bay Region house are ...equally symbolic."

However, it is for the mid-19th century's champion of the Gothic Revival, Alexander James Beresford Beresford-Hope, to most clearly describe the aspirations of many of his age, and, far from coincidentally, what would become those of the Bay Region style's earliest practitioners. Under the banner of "Progressive Eclecticism," in an 1862 issue of *The Ecclesiologist*, Hope writes, "what we hope to develop is a type of art ... which though called medieval, is still modern and progressive."

Eclecticism, a vulgarity to the old International Stylists and their current day kin, runs through the entire history of the Bay Region style, from Maybeck's Gothic, to Wurster's farmhouses, to Charles Moore and William Turnbull's barns, to Jeremy Kotas' borrowings from the style's earlier architects.

Moore, writing in *Bay Area Houses*, describes the mid-twentieth-century American arc of historical borrowing: "in the decades after World War II, the most malevolent adjective available for architect's use was eclectic ... so that by the forties architects sat at their drawing boards, confident that their every line was a clean one, unsullied by previous use ... In the sixties, and especially in the early seventies, an increasing degree of candor allows us to admit that we have actually looked at existing places."

The Bay Region style is not a Style

For more than fifty years, attempts have been made to define the Bay Region style, aka Bay Area Tradition, aka Bay Area Style, aka Bay Area school. Some have proposed that it is a matter of form, scale, materials, sources, and preferences. Others suggest it has to do with history. Others, still, are certain that it is a kind of native variation on the country's mainstream domestic architectural production. And, of course, some have denied its existence, though many of these seem never to have visited the Bay Area.

I wonder if they aren't all correct, even these last.

The Bay Region style is hardly a Style. It has no constituent architectonic elements (though certain motives and styles re-cur more than others) and no characteristic plan (though both interior and exterior arrangements are often informal). In fact, Bay Region style houses have been rendered in almost the full range of architectural styles. In the pages following are houses gotten up in English Arts and Crafts, as the ruin of an Irish tower, in English and French Gothic, French storybook and Monterey Style, Organic and International Style, Japanese, "Mineshaft Modern" and Spanish Colonial Revival, Victorian, Post-Modern and Neo-Primitive, High Tech, and, what else?, Bay Region style. Most of these houses conform to some definition of the style, though some don't.

What is similar from Bay Region house to Bay Region house, I think, is the way each architect has puzzled out the design; and I think this is only a little different from what Beresford-Hope had in mind 150 years ago. While he meant to make new architecture from strictly medieval ingredients, Bay Region architects, since the late nineteenth century, have sought "modern and progressive" houses employing the full range of architectural sources. This is eclecticism of a different sort than often practiced. For Bay Region architects, as for Beresford-Hope, eclecticism is not the goal, but a means to making new architecture. Among these architects, there is almost no interest in verbatim reproductions or simple revivals of house styles. Wurster's farm houses are impossible to confuse with those in the Central Valley. Maybeck's Gothic is never "correct." Though some historians point to these architects' embrace of "Yankee" sources, the ur-Yankee house Style — American colonial revival — is almost never attempted by Bay Region architects. The Style is too inelastic and confining, impossible to make new.

For these architects, unlike the heroes of architectural Modernism, innovation stands on the shoulders of history. Howard Roark was no Bay Area architect.

The invention of the Bay Region style, what makes it different from the architecture of other places, lies just in this strange stew of Romanticism, eclecticism, and the Picturesque; progressivism and modernity; "take-a-chance clients, mild, even climate, no insects or bugs, ... and the immensity of the scene." If, as Mordaunt Crook suggests, the Picturesque occasions eclecticism, perhaps we should describe the Bay Region style as Picturesque Modernism, a reconciliation of words long thought opposed. ■

Charles Moore House, Orinda, 1962, Morley Baer photographer. TOP Exterior with sliding walls closed. BOTTOM Interior with sliding doors open.
Images courtesy Morley Baer Photography Trust.

Bernard Maybeck

Bernard Maybeck, portrait.

In his 1988 forward to the then new edition of *Bay Area Houses*, David Gebhard presciently predicted that "designers of the near future will turn their attention to the (Bay Area) Tradition's second phase, finding a new source of inspiration in the open romanticism and easy-going quality of the work of the latter thirties and forties." There has been renewed interest, especially, in the signal architect of this period, William Wurster. This culminated, in 1995, the centenary of Wurster's birth, with the San Francisco Museum of Modern Art's exhibition "An Everyday Modernism: the Houses of William Wurster," accompanied by an excellent, alike-titled, volume.

Almost utterly absent, strangely, is appreciation for Wurster's talented peers, including John Dinwiddie, John Funk, Francis Joseph McCarthy, and, especially, Gardner Dailey, whose elegant, masterful houses are overdue for critical re-appraisal. Will this happen before every last one of them is either demolished or "improved" into oblivion?

With all this, and despite the almost fifty years since his death, the towering figure of the Bay Region style remains Bernard Maybeck.

While being shown around one of the newer houses included here, I noted quite literal quotations from Wurster and Moore. On asking the architect about these, I was met with a blank, though probably not hostile, stare, and assured that the only influence at work in this way was Maybeck's.

In *An Everyday Modernism*, Marc Treib writes "Thus, in their regard for the climate, materials, and site, and in their free interpretation of history and precedent, Maybeck's houses were the direct precursors of those by William Wurster." It's an unexpected comparison. The two sets of houses appear very different — Wurster's "Yankee" work with Maybeck's, whose sources are almost always European. And the rhetorical distance between the two — from Wurster's modernism to Maybeck's eclecticism — is often thought considerable. However, it is a distance that many, including architects and historians, critics and curators, are willing to travel, to reconcile their efforts with a fellow Charles Keeler described this way in his typescript "Friends Bearing Torches": "His eyes were dark and his expression was benign... Instead of a vest, he wore a sash, and his suit seemed like a homespun of a dark brown color...The serenity and self-possession of his manner was disarming, his unique point of view, so confidently held, was at once irritating and stimulating. Here was a benign young Socrates..."

He arranged small-scale pageants, worked informally and unconventionally, got his hands dirty with cement and paint, wrote poetically and enigmatically, was a poor businessman but affable bohemian, who inspired the many drawn to him, and, often, wore a beret. He's yin to the yang of Frank Lloyd Wright, to whom many, including Mumford, have compared Maybeck. He was a Romantic artist whose houses are art. The Bay Area historian and critic Grey Brechin describes dwelling in a Maybeck house as "like living in a Monet."

Is it any wonder that Maybeck, together with his work, is such an irresistible model? Subsequent generations of Bay Region architects have built their own houses, written abstractly, and floundered financially while cultivating distinctive personalities, even if they could not quite bring themselves to adopt artistic French headwear. While the houses assembled here are hardly a scientific sample, it is significant that many of them fall outside the usual paradigm — houses designed by architects for clients. Nearly a third are designed by architects and artists for themselves.

Maybeck's example was almost immediately compelling. Many of the Bay Region style's earliest practitioners included here were directly associated with Maybeck. Willis Polk and John Hudson Thomas were his students; and Polk remained his friend. Ernest Coxhead employed him. Julia Morgan was both his student and, later, collaborator on projects administered through her office. He designed a house for Lilian Bridgman, who was so taken with it that she gave up teaching physics and took up the study of architecture.

In fact, this sort of web of relationships has been characteristic of Bay Region architects throughout the style's history, and accounts in some measure for its continuity. The degrees of separation among those discussed in the following pages never rises as high as six.

For example, Maybeck collaborator Julia Morgan, also an acquaintance of Lilian Bridgman's, employed Gardner Dailey, who worked with his later competitor William Wurster in the office of John Galen Howard. Wurster wrote about Polk, Coxhead, and Maybeck, and headed the College of Environmental Design at U. C. Berkeley. The College was later led by Joseph Esherick, who had worked in Dailey's office, and whose firm employed Laura Hartman, who, with her partner Richard Fernau, have both taught at the College. Charles Moore was Chairman of the Architecture Department, and partnered with William Turnbull, Donlyn Lyndon, and Richard Whitaker. Lyndon, too, was Department Chair. Others who have taught in the College include Claude Stoller, Mark Mack, Mary Griffin, Lucia Howard and myself (Ace Architects). And yes, Charles Moore was my uncle.

There are, of course, many other strands in this web, though their effect is identical. An interesting footnote, though, is that very few of these Bay Region-style architects are from the Bay Region. Most have come early in their careers, then been unwilling to leave.

With this book, the intention was to open up the meaning of the Bay Region style, and cast a very wide net. Toward this we've included several mid-twentieth-century houses which probably once seemed wholly Internationally Styled, but have in the intervening 50 or so years softened sufficiently to now appear "Bay Regional." Also included are several houses designed, and built, by artists for themselves (by artist, I mean artist, not beret-topped architect). These may well lie beyond the boundary line. Yet, these "artistic" houses are so similar in so many ways to the earliest Bay Region-style houses, that we could not exclude them.

Of course, the great majority of the houses following are unquestionably Bay Region style, and many of these can only be counted the usual suspects. Here. again, we feel the long reach of Maybeck, pointing us to familiar territory. It is an irony that the Bay Area's distinctive domestic style is provided by a relative handful of its houses.

A further irony is that relatively few of the Bay Area's many architects choose to work in the local style. A consequence is that residential work by several fine local architects is not included in the following pages.

Whither

In 1976, writing in *Bay Area Houses*, Charles Moore wondered if the Bay Region style had run its course. "The fifteen years since 1960 form a separate chapter, the third and perhaps final act in the drama of a special Bay Area architecture. If it is an obituary, it is a strangely uncertain one: did the Bay Area Tradition ever, in fact, exist? Is it gone? Or perhaps alive and well but somewhere else?"

Yet, by 1988 and the book's reprinting, its editor Sally Woodbridge reports that "the decade from 1976 to the late eighties has shown — to paraphrase Mark Twain — that the reports of the tradition's death have been highly exaggerated." She deploys several houses to make the point, including one designed by Moore. She notes an important change, though, one that jeopardizes the tradition of small 'artistic' houses designed by architects for themselves and others: "the Tradition's elitist quality, ... noted by Gebhard, is increasingly based on wealth alone. An educated preference for the simple life rooted in the land is much less likely to influence current taste in the design of houses than it did in previous generations — never mind that apparently 'simple houses' now take what was once a fortune to build." Recall that this was written well before the latest run-up in Bay Area residential real estate.

Those peering into the future of the Bay Region style have assembled a mixed record (truth be told, they are almost never right). Still, let's consider three recent houses that may suggest the path ahead.

All are modestly-sized, especially by contemporary, super-sized standards. Each is conventionally built, more or less, unlike the involved, Jetson-y constructions of the current, nostalgic International Style Revival. None occupy the dramatic sites once abundant in the Bay Area, but all make the most of their respective locations.

All, I would argue, are progressively eclectic, reaching back various distances and directions into architecture's history in order to fashion modern and, yes, "progressive" dwellings.

The design of a tiny addition to a small, 1940s, builder's house near Berkeley (Top right row) was provoked by the owners' attending a lecture about grand, eighteenth- and nineteenth-century Mexican haciendas. On the ride home they realized they could build something like the places they'd just seen. Their re-worked house now features its sources' characteristic courtyard, verandah, and tower, in extreme miniature. The tower is so petite it doesn't contain an upper floor, just openings funneling and reflecting daylight into the space below. That the entire ensemble recalls Wurster's 1928 Gregory Farmhouse, which itself relied on similar sources, is hardly coincidence.

Some might not suspect that this diminutive, far from high style, Berkeley cottage (Middle right row) was designed by architects at all. There's the matter of its walls being made of old license plates, for example. Yet, in the age of recycling, what used to be a backwoodsman's building material of last resort is, now, also the latest expression of ecological responsibility. Either way, the effect could hardly be more picturesque. Unlike most rural shanties, the house's interior rises upwards to the light.

With this eccentric, not large, up-to-the-minute Sonoma Valley farmhouse (Bottom right row), artist/architects Bruce Tomb and John Randolph nonetheless harken back to early Bay Region style "artistic" dwellings. In fact, art concepts permeate this house, and critical components were hand-made and finished by the architects, a la Maybeck. The imagery of the place is simultaneously right-now and antique (progressive and eclectic). What does the roof form resemble, if not a gambrel barn cocked to one side? ■

TOP Littlejohn House, Kensington, addition 1982, Donlyn Lyndon.
MIDDLE Hester/McNally Residence, Berkeley, 1999, Arkin Tilt Architects.
BOTTOM C House, Sonoma, 1998, Bruce Tomb and John Randolph.

Willis Polk **Polk-Willams House** San Francisco 1892

At the front of this double house, designed for the painter Mrs. Virgil Williams and for Polk's family, two eccentrically-shaped dark-shingled bays, looking like the slightly sinister houses of working folk in German Expressionist movies, appear to pitch out towards the narrow pedestrian path at the edge of Russian Hill. (Historians guess that Polk's source may have been certain medieval French houses.) The gable end of the larger (Williams) bay features a Gothicized window; while a very steeply sloping roof sits atop the small (Polk) bay like a witch's hat — an effect enhanced by the flare at the roof's brim and two tiny square windows, like eyes, set just below.

At the back, this pair of houses is an impromptu-looking assemblage of porches, decks, and windows of every size and proportion, cascading over the hill's precipice, and down five stories.

Inside, individual spaces are small, except when they are very small, or smaller still. Ingenuities of scale, especially at the top floor, prevent a feeling of confinement. Indeed, the effect is of a kind of Bohemian rusticity seen especially in the contrast

between the rough redwood roof framing and highly finished redwood wall paneling, doors, railings, and other interior fittings.

In response to those unnerved by the house's appearance, Polk painted this motto on one of a set of panels over the sitting room fireplace: "Was Kummerts den Mond das due Hunde Bellen?" — What does the moon care if the wolves howl at it? ∎

OPPOSITE Polk House sitting room with painted wood panels above fireplace.

ABOVE Polk's House is to the left, Williams' to the right.

Polk House

OPPOSITE
Polk House staircase. Fireplace
hearth is last stair tread and,
around the corner, a low bench.

ABOVE LEFT
Living room, Polk House.

ABOVE RIGHT
Dining room.

OPPOSITE
Staircase to loft above living room.

ABOVE LEFT
Classically styled clock in loft above
Polk House sitting room.

ABOVE RIGHT
Bedroom.

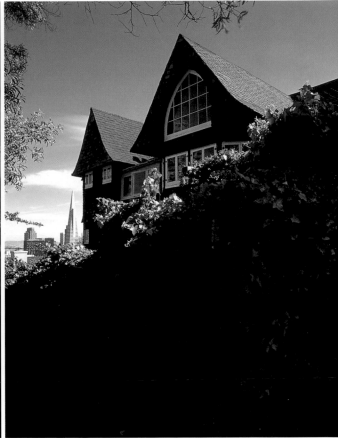

Willlams House

OPPOSITE
Brick fireplace and redwood casework with exposed roof framing.

ABOVE LEFT
High, Gothicized window and low window seat, fitted across faceted bay.

ABOVE RIGHT
View of both houses at crest of Russian Hill.

ABOVE LEFT
Bohemian rusticity — Sitting room
with loft above to the right. Very
low rail is rendered as a classical
building facade.

ABOVE RIGHT
Bedroom, more rustic than
Bohemian — common brick
fireplace, redwood board walls,
exposed ceiling framing.

OPPOSITE
Bedroom.

Ernest Coxhead Coxhead House San Francisco 1893

Though less rustic (and spooky) than his friend Willis Polk's place, Ernest Coxhead's nearly contemporaneous Pacific Heights dwelling is similarly eccentric. The end of this house overhangs a tall concrete wall and, like Polk's, is a large, shingled bay with a steeply sloping pitched roof. A corner window without precedent (or sequel for that matter) is this street facade's most diverting feature.

The entire effect is of English Arts and Crafts without the stifling decorum. We can imagine how well this suited Coxhead, an Englishman transplanted to California.

It is the path through the house, though, wide and narrow, careering along the edges of some rooms, and through the middle of others — a kind of dark ride of the early Bay Region style — that is the singular achievement here. The historian John Beach, in *Bay Area Houses*,

describes it this way, "It is as if the house had been trimmed away, leaving only the circulation space. Then a step here and a landing there are extruded horizontally, expanded from a small space to a larger. By this curious process the stair sequence ceases to be simply an element of a larger building, but is transformed into the building itself." ■

OPPOSITE Street facade with shingled bay overhanging rough stucco wall.

ABOVE LEFT Path to front door.

ABOVE RIGHT Garden facade.

OPPOSITE
Living room with large redwood fireplace surround, partially hidden high window to its right, and carefully finished redwood beam ceiling.

ABOVE LEFT
Large fireplace by the front door opens to wide hall.

ABOVE RIGHT
Long redwood gallery leading from foyer to rear garden.

ABOVE LEFT
Dining room looking into
conservatory-like gallery.

ABOVE MIDDLE
Bedroom with exposed beams
is open to the steep gable of the
roof.

ABOVE RIGHT
Hall opens to two-story redwood
stairwell. Mysterious stair to third
floor spills into hall.

OPPOSITE
Dining room with large windows to
the garden and built-in redwood
cabinets.

Bernard Maybeck **Roos House** San Francisco 1909

This Presidio Heights house is variously described, by historians, as English Tudor, Arts and Crafts, and French/English Gothic. The place includes fireplaces styled Renaissance and red silk electric lanterns, which can only be called Chinese. Critics judge it "most urbane" and "erratic." It is a large, complex, ornate house designed by an architect famous for, among other things, dwellings that are small and, allegedly, simple.

The Roos House was a wedding present, provided by the Orpheum Theater magnate Morris Meyerfeld to his daughter Elizabeth. She hired Bernard Maybeck, whose great champion was Charles Keeler, author of *The Simple House* (1904), and ardent follower of the Socialist William Morris. However, if Maybeck, his Socialist confreres just across the Bay, felt any reluctance at working for a merchant prince of hyper-capitalism, it does not show here.

The Roos House is unflinchingly luxe. Kenneth Cardwell, in his *Bernard Maybeck*, describes the interior — "Panels of mauve plush edged with gold gimp harmonize with redwood walls. Redwood battens and moldings have Gothic profiles… Wall coverings, light fixtures, and furniture — even the heraldic crest of the owner's initials ornamenting the front door — were fashioned from designs by Maybeck." ■

OPPOSITE Street-facing bay with overscaled Gothic tracery rendered in painted wood.

ABOVE View from street with redwood columned loggia leading to front door.

ABOVE RIGHT Front door with Maybeck-designed crest.

OPPOSITE
Great room with Maybeck-
designed furniture adjacent to
great Renaissance-inspired
fireplace. Clusters of floating
light bulbs hang from painted
chandeliers.

ABOVE LEFT
Dining room from entry hall —
velvet lined doors are set against
redwood walls and beamed
ceiling.

ABOVE RIGHT
Dining room, looking toward great
hall.

ABOVE LEFT
Redwood stairwell emerges into
plaster-finished corridor.

ABOVE RIGHT
Private sitting room adjacent to
upstairs bedrooms.

OPPOSITE
Sitting room adjacent to great hall.

Julia Morgan **McCormac House** Berkeley 1911

She designed the most famous house in California, for its most public citizen, yet pursued anonymity. She designed and saw built more than seven hundred buildings; but "She generally avoided social gatherings, participation in professional groups, or in women's organizations, and shunned publicity of any kind, including the architectural press" writes Richard Longstreth, in *The Architecture of Julia Morgan*. It is also said she burned her papers and drawings upon retirement — a myth fueled by her social reluctance. She is a sort of Greta Garbo of the Bay Region style — an early star architect who nonetheless wanted to be left alone.

In the 1988 *Julia Morgan, Architect*, her biographer, and occasional booster, Sara Boutelle, describes Morgan's houses this way — "Her primary weakness in domestic architecture was a lack of boldness, but that was what pleased her clients." It is for historian John Beach to connect the dots, seeing in Morgan's work parallels with her personality — "She seems to have altered Vitruvius in some subtle way: firmness,

commodity, and propriety were her watchwords…in fact, the aspect of vernacular design which appealed most to Morgan was its anonymity. All the Bay Area practitioners seem to have had a fascination with the vernacular to some degree, but of them all, only Morgan produced buildings which … were actually indistinguishable from those of an earnest carpenter."

This handsome, modest, carefully designed and well-made Berkeley house, built for a university professor whose budget did not extend to $5,000, is a quiet landmark. ∎

OPPOSITE A redwood-board bay projects from the tall brown shingle house toward the street. Decorative, leaded-glass windows are set in an architectural frame.

ABOVE LEFT Entry from covered porch.

ABOVE RIGHT Stair hall from foyer.

OPPOSITE
View to living room. Highly finished
redwood beams at ceiling lead
toward bay window.

ABOVE
An unusual double window seat
fills the front bay.

ABOVE
Wood-cased fireplace in dining
room.

OPPOSITE
Dining room from foyer.

Robinson Jeffers **Tor House** Carmel 1919

California poet Robinson Jeffers and his new wife, Una, arrived in Carmel in 1914, expecting a short stay until the War's end, planning to make their home in England. As the War continued, plans changed, and by 1919 work was complete on Tor House, the first of a series of buildings Jeffers built with his own hands on a bluff overlooking Monterey Bay. It was a project the poet pursued until his death, more than forty years later.

The form of the house is taken from an ancient English barn Una recalled, and built of large, smooth stones pulled up from the beach below. Hawk Tower, completed in 1925, is modeled on a ruined castle, and, like the house, recreates a setting from "the sceptered isle," Una and Robinson's destination, before War intervened. ■

OPPOSITE Hawk Tower to the left with Tor House to the right.

ABOVE RIGHT Tor House with the original cottage in front, dining room and kitchen additions and renovations beyond are later.

Near the end of his life, Jeffers, in this excerpt from "The Last Conservative," described Tor House:

> Against the outcrop boulders of a raised beach
> We built our house when I and my love were young.
> Here long ago the surf thundered, now fifty feet lower;
> And there's a kind of shell-mound, I used to see ghosts of Indians
> Squatting beside the stones in their firelight,
> The rock-cheeks have red fire-stains. But the place was maiden, no previous
> Building, no neighbors, nothing but the elements,
> Rock, wind, and sea; in moon-struck nights the mountain coyotes
> Howled in our dooryard; or doe and fawn
> Stared in the lamp-lit window. We raised two boys here;
>   All that we saw or heard was beautiful
> And hardly human.

OPPOSITE & ABOVE LEFT
Living room with low redwood
beam ceiling.

ABOVE MIDDLE
Steep redwood stair leads to
bedrooms upstairs.

ABOVE RIGHT
Nook at base of stairs, with Una's
desk.

ABOVE LEFT
Opening near living room fireplace
leads to bedroom.

OPPOSITE
Bedroom.

ABOVE MIDDLE
Dining room with gallery
reached by a trap door, where
children could play without being
underfoot.

ABOVE RIGHT
Bust of Jeffers at dining room and
view to kitchen beyond.

ABOVE
Una's room in Hawk Tower,
wood paneled with deep Gothic
windows.

OPPOSITE
Hawk Tower with oriel window.

John Hudson Thomas **Hume Cloister** Berkeley 1928

Outside, it's a Spanish castle, with gently sloping clay-tile roofs and high, thick, masonry walls, punctuated by small, irregularly placed, variously styled windows. David Gebhard, in *Bay Area Houses*, describes the place — "One's traditional sense of scale is denied in such buildings, … it appears to be a distant, not quite believable stone castle … high on a mountainous crag." Inside, the place is Gothic. At its center is a medieval cloister, a half-size miniature of its fourteenth-century model in Toulouse, France. Groin-vaulted passageways, secret staircases,

and great, stone fireplaces fuel the effect.

The Humes, Portia Bell and Bill, appear to have been a modern power couple. She was among the earliest West Coast Freudians, and a remarkable beauty, photographed by Imogen Cunningham, among others. He was director of the university's Greek Theatre and established the Berkeley campus art museum.

Together, they traveled in France for several years, surveying scores of medieval buildings in preparation for the design of

their Berkeley house. In the ferociously eclectic John Hudson Thomas, whose enthusiasm for joining un-like architectural elements and masterful eye for scale and telling detail make him, perhaps, the most underappreciated of early Bay Region-style architects, the Humes found the perfect raconteur of their European travels. ■

OPPOSITE Terrace off living room with steel glass doors set in cast concrete Gothic tracery.

ABOVE LEFT Castellated stair tower.

ABOVE RIGHT Massive walls of hilltop cloister seen from street below.

OPPOSITE
Concrete block walls are made
from material quarried in cast on
site.

ABOVE LEFT
Front door with cast concrete
Gothic door surround set into
block stone archway.

ABOVE RIGHT
Exterior walls include openings in
several architectural styles.

OPPOSITE

Wood beam ceilings; block walls;
carved wood doors; casework and
furniture; and terra cotta tile floors.

ABOVE LEFT

Groin-vaulted tile and block foyer.

ABOVE RIGHT

Living room with open block stair
to book lined gallery above.

ABOVE LEFT
View of cloister through large
steel sash window.

ABOVE RIGHT
Dining room with over-scaled
fireplace.

OPPOSITE
Cloister — a half-size miniature
of a fourteenth-century French
monastery.

W. R. Yelland Normandy Village Berkeley 1928

Returning World War I veteran Walter Raymond Yelland opened his architectural practice in 1917. He had served in France, and by 1921 was writing enthusiastically about "The Auvergne Village" in *Architect and Engineer*.

This hyper-picturesque cluster of apartments is the apogee of Yelland's imaginative recastings of rural, medieval France, as well as the landmark of the storybook strain of the Bay Region style.

The Bay Area in the 1920s, was a hotbed of storybook houses whose architects included, in addition to Yelland, Carr Jones and Hugh Comstock.

Normandy Village and the Hume Cloister (p.55), built in the same year, share much in common. Both are based on medieval European models, and rely on breathtaking jumps in scale, among other arresting devices, for their effect.

Still, these are fundamentally different places. Yelland's apartments, drawn from a single source, form a kind of romantic stage set. Thomas' castle, on the other hand, radically recombines disparate elements from architecture's history, chosen for their rich and provocative emotional associations. In this way, Thomas' work, like Maybeck's, achieves just that gravity and modernity which Normandy Village so successfully overcomes. ∎

OPPOSITE Stepped plaster gable at courtyard.

ABOVE LEFT Medieval cluster from street with wood-shingle roofs, half-timber plaster, over a rough brick base. Over-scaled archway leads to a series of courtyards.

ABOVE RIGHT Rear courtyard and paths to several apartments — each unit has a unique plan and entry.

ABOVE LEFT
View from foyer to dining room.

ABOVE MIDDLE
Bedroom.

ABOVE RIGHT
Fireplace inglenook and brick
windowseat.

OPPOSITE
Living room with rustic brick
"beehive" fireplace and rough
plaster walls.

Lilian Bridgman Wills Hunting Lodge Lafayette 1930

This house, called a hunting lodge in its day, is set on several once remote acres east of Berkeley. The floor plan is simple — two rooms to either side of a first floor dog trot with sleeping quarters above. Yet, the place is enthusiastically designed and densely eclectic.

A two-story porch facing distant Mt. Diablo is rendered Monterey Colonial. Redwood board and batten siding and interior paneling is Arts and Crafts. The clay-tile roofing, terra-cotta pavers, and interior ceramic tilework is Spanish Colonial; while horizontal window mullions whisper Streamline Moderne.

It is no surprise, then, that this architect's teacher was Bernard Maybeck, who helped Bridgman design her Berkeley home in 1900. The experience, apparently, was transformative. She gave up teaching physics and undertook architecture, while remaining active in a variety of artistic pursuits.

Of course, this was no hunting lodge. Clarence Wills, a prominent San Francisco-peninsula physician, built the place as a hideaway for his mistress and himself; and it included a small outbuilding, to which the mistress repaired when the doctor invited friends (to preserve the fiction, in a time when appearances mattered, that she was the housekeeper). ∎

OPPOSITE Two-story redwood verandah facing cactus garden.

ABOVE LEFT Redwood board and batten siding sits atop a red brick first story. Handmade clay tiles cover the roof.

ABOVE RIGHT The site is an archetypal California landscape of rolling grass-covered foothills, with views to Mr. Diablo in the distance.

OPPOSITE
Glass doors fold away opening
the dog-trot hall to verandah and
garden. Tile pavers at the hall
step down to sandstone blocks
at the terrace.

ABOVE LEFT
Twelve-by-twelve redwood timbers
case doorways and windows.

ABOVE MIDDLE
Living room with hand-forged
lights and ceramic tile mural over
fireplace.

ABOVE RIGHT
Smooth redwood board and batten
walls at the dining room.

ABOVE LEFT
View to bedroom upper floor hall.

ABOVE RIGHT
Ceramic tile "Turkish carpet" in
a colorful tile field in bathroom.

OPPOSITE
Bedroom with redwood board
and batten walls and ceiling.

Gardner Dailey **Heil Residence** San Francisco 1941

In 1967, after more than forty years as a San Francisco architect, Gardner Dailey ended it all in an especially regional way, flinging himself from the Golden Gate Bridge. He had established his practice in 1926, the same year William Wurster set up shop. For the next quarter century, they were the Bay Area's pre-eminent residential architects. Yet, while Wurster's star still burns brightly, Dailey, now, is largely forgotten.

This small Pacific Heights house, designed for Walter Heil, director of the deYoung Museum, was built on the eve of America's entry into World War II. Elegant and apparently simple, it prefigures, with almost eerie precision, much that would be found in houses built in the war's wake.

In the catalog to the 1949 exhibition "Domestic Architecture of the San Francisco Bay Region" (the show occasioned by Mumford's "little attempt at reporting what was happening in the outside world"), Dailey wrote "…we note the disappearance of the Large House, and in its place the appearance of what may be termed, 'The Large-Small House'," which "has one very large room, and the balance of the house has been compressed wherever possible." Walter Heil's "large-small house" anticipated this development eight years and a World War earlier. ∎

OPPOSITE Painted vertical board facade from entry courtyard.

ABOVE Ground level courtyard extends over garage at street.

ABOVE LEFT
Streamline Moderne curvilinear
stair.

ABOVE MIDDLE
White plaster-finished living room,
from dining area.

ABOVE RIGHT
Dining room beyond over-scaled
windows, with original suspended
light fixture.

OPPOSITE
Living room with glazed porch
overlooking front courtyard

Francis Joseph McCarthy Kellogg House San Francisco 1948

Perched on a steep corner site on the northern slope of Potrero Hill, this small dwelling is largely hidden from passersby. The single exception is a large, louvered bay, whose long, wide fins suggest some hidden purpose.

Inside the wall surrounding the place is a surprisingly large, surprisingly sunny garden on two levels, surrounded by the house, on two sides. Adhering to Dailey's formulation of the Post-War dwelling — the Large-Small House — public areas are contained in a single generous volume, adjacent to the garden, with a panoramic prospect toward the City.

The fins line the street side of the living room, and are adjustable with a crank, frustrating the nosy and widening the view.

The Kellogs, it seems, were a no-nonsense couple, ideal for an Internationally-Styled, Post-War house. When asked to comment, in the 1961 *Contemporary Houses Evaluated by their Owners*, they responded "Our requirements were a 'soft-modern' house (hence the shingles on the exterior and the pine plywood inside), privacy without curtaining or blinds, ceilings as high as we could afford (obtained through a shed roof plan), fireplaces,…a separate kitchen, ample storage."

Clearly, for the Kellogs, unlike earlier Bay Region house clients, Gothic would not have done. ■

OPPOSITE Adjustable vertical wood fins permit views, ensure privacy.

ABOVE From across the street, the fins entirely shield the living room from the view of those passing by.

OPPOSITE
Floating fireplace at living room
with view of San Francisco and
Bay Bridge.

ABOVE
Interior courtyard and garden
on two levels.

ABOVE LEFT
Mantle with asymmetrical display cases over black marble hearth.

ABOVE RIGHT
Large wood exterior fins adjust to modulate light and privacy.

OPPOSITE
Interior courtyard from dining room.

Jack Hillmer Munger House Napa 1950

If, in the late 1940s, on a warm summer evening in the Napa Valley, Frank Lloyd Wright had clambered into a hot tub, a tumbler of chardonnay in one hand and a pencil and sketchbook in the other, he might have drawn a house like this one. Since Wright didn't, though, it was left for Jack Hillmer.

At its front, two converging concrete block walls funnel you to the small front door. Inside, to your left, a twisting passage leads toward the large living/kitchen/dining room. To your right, the bedroom is reached through either the shower or toilet room, your choice. It's a space-saving idea whose time awaits.

Opaque at its front, the house is all glass at its back edge, curling around the end of an extensive lawn, whose edges are shaded by oaks. While the plan marches along to the pattern of parallelograms incised in the floor; the roof is like some fantastical abstract origami — twisting and folding; rising and falling; projecting, hovering, and receding in strange, masterful ways. ■

OPPOSITE At the garden, the exterior wall is made entirely of glass set between wooden posts.

ABOVE LEFT Floor and roof extend past the glass wall at living room.

ABOVE RIGHT Ribbon windows separate walls and roof at entry.

ABOVE LEFT
Window seat along block walls
wraps around fireplace toward
garden front. Concrete floor is
scored in a diamond pattern.

ABOVE RIGHT
Interior and exterior walls adhere to
the strict geometry scribed into the
floor. Here, a view of the faceted
kitchen counter.

ABOVE LEFT
Bedroom wing.

ABOVE RIGHT
Interior passageway to bedrooms
through either shower or toilet room.

Nathaniel Owings **Wild Bird** Big Sur 1957

At a distance, this small house, really a species of cabin, is hardly distinguishable from the rocky promontory on which it rests, at the edge of the continent, the Pacific Ocean six hundred feet below.

Robinson Jeffers set much of his poetry along the Big Sur coast, seized by the connection, he thought inextricable, between overwhelming natural beauty and human tragedy.

Margaret Owings, who built this house with her architect-husband Nathaniel (the "O" in SOM, or Skidmore, Owings & Merrill) and architect Mark Mills, was more interested in sea otters, though hardly immune to the place's contemplative pull. Interviewed by critic Paul Goldberger for a 1996 article in *Architectural Digest*, she observes "Big Sur intensifies everything. I think of looking down its coast as looking down the centuries…" Goldberger continues, describing the house — a "tiny tent of wood and glass" and its interior — "a kind of modernist grotto; defined by dark wood and bright glass, it is both enveloping and open to the world. Embodying this contradiction is Margaret Owings herself… A silver-haired woman of stunning elegance, she is the mix of aristocrat and bohemian that once flourished in California, and it is not hard to imagine her growing up in the Berkeley of Bernard Maybeck and Julia Morgan." ∎

OPPOSITE The "tiny tent of wood and glass" is barely discernible.

ABOVE As its name suggests, Wild Bird perches on the edge of the precipice.

OPPOSITE
Massive concrete frames cast on
site support the roof of the main
living space and allow areas of
walls and roof to be constructed
of glass.

ABOVE LEFT
Rock quarried nearby forms the
fireplace wall and long, raised
hearth.

ABOVE RIGHT
Open kitchen.

OPPOSITE
Bedroom wing. View from south
terrace.

ABOVE
South terrace seat built along
(unnervingly) low redwood railing.
Rounded rocks were set into the
concrete deck in a variety of patterns
and textures by the Owings.

ABOVE LEFT
Bathroom with view toward
Pacific Ocean.

ABOVE RIGHT
Margaret Owings' bedroom.

OPPOSITE
Quintessential Big Sur view down
the coast from the bedroom.

Warren Callister **Flowers House** Berkeley 1958

When Lewis Mumford observed, in his incendiary 1947 *New Yorker* article, that the Bay Region "style is actually a product of the meeting of Oriental and Occidental architectural traditions," I wonder if he had houses like this in mind.

The following year, Warren Callister completed the first of a series of Japanese houses in Berkeley, of which the Flowers House is the last, and most refined. From below, it appears distant, its size strangely indeterminate, like castles in Edo period Japanese wood block prints. Inside, the house is a series of precisely-scaled rooms, each at its own level, interlocked by a dazzlingly complex staircase. Steel sash windows take on the character of shojis. The place is meticulously crafted, and is experienced as a great serene cabinet.

In 1950, writing in the *Western Architect and Engineer*, Callister offered that "My concern is not with recreating the old, but rather with creating our own unique eclecticism." The Japanese house was a source for a variety of Bay Area architects, through to the late 1950s when, as David Gebhard notes in Bay Area Houses, "it was evident that the practitioners of the tradition were groping for new images, which could revitalize what had become tired."

Among those leading this revitalization in the 1960s was Charles Moore, whose first house for himself, in 1954, had been styled Japanese. ∎

OPPOSITE View from below.

ABOVE LEFT Entry with vertical boards, plaster panels, and steel sash.

ABOVE RIGHT View from street.

ABOVE LEFT
Foyer and adjacent stair.

OPPOSITE
View down the center of elegant
complex stair.

ABOVE MIDDLE
Highly crafted stair rises several
floors.

ABOVE RIGHT
Top level of stairway with overlook
to below.

OPPOSITE
Living room with steel sash
windows detailed to resemble
shoji screens.

ABOVE LEFT & MIDDLE
Views along house with wooden
railings and decks.

ABOVE RIGHT
Kitchen from dining room.

ABOVE
Family room at lowest floor, with
redwood walls, concrete fireplace
and hearth, and steel sash.

OPPOSITE
Built-in casework and strategically
positioned mirror at bedroom.

Joseph Esherick McLeod House Belvedere 1962

Charles Moore's "Action House," which appeared in the April 1965, *Architectural Forum* is both an apt description of this house, as well as of principles and people he then admired. The following is an excerpt.

"Esherick's houses ... use the instant analytical techniques of the painter, especially the action painter... The McLeod house, on the top of Belvedere Island overlooking San Francisco Bay, is a strong case in point. There is the sense that this architect plunged down the steep hill past the oak to the marine view,

gobbled it all up, and brought forth the house in chunks of light and outlook — the way the action painter flinging his wet paint onto his canvas, responds directly to it in whatever way the ensuing seconds seem to demand.

"This is not to say that the McLeod house is careless: the detailing is meticulous, the workmanship neat, the range of materials and colors austerely disciplined, the strict budget carefully adhered to, and the attention to domestic comforts complete. It's just that the

house maintains a permanent sense of casually exploding into its site.

"The explosion is so casual, so easy to take, that Mrs. McLeod doesn't notice it any more, until she goes to anyone else's house and feels imprisoned." ∎

OPPOSITE View to San Francisco Bay.

ABOVE LEFT Low-key and slightly overgrown, the entry leads round a large oak, offering no hint of the vista beyond the door.

ABOVE RIGHT The trellis-topped deck extends the space of the dining room.

ABOVE LEFT
View from foyer towards dining room.

OPPOSITE
High-ceilinged entry hall with signature Esherick skylight.

ABOVE MIDDLE
View towards entry. The wooden ceiling was laminated by the owner from two-by-fours.

ABOVE RIGHT
Generous wood stairs lead up into the living room and again to the entry hall.

ABOVE LEFT
Kitchen.

ABOVE RIGHT
Bathroom.

OPPOSITE
The solid shingled house
dissolves at the end, where the
tall sitting room is like an elegant
conservatory.

Marquis & Stoller Pence House Mill Valley 1962

Like Wildbird, the chief part of this house's substantial magic arises from its site, which, even if it's not the meeting of the North American continent and the planet's greatest ocean but only a blufftop in Marin County, is certainly spectacular enough. Coupled with the informal arrangement of its four, Japanese-like pavilions (as well as non-stop, worldwide publication), the house became, for a time, a romantic icon for a certain easygoing way of life in Northern California in the 1960s.

Charles Moore, in *Bay Area Houses*, saw in the place echoes of Louis Kahn's bath houses in Trenton, New Jersey, an icon of a wholly different order; and noted that the Pence "plan shows that the pavilions are simply divided into the rooms one would expect in a not-very-large dwelling…" Yet, if the plan is conventional, the house's assemblage of apparently discrete little buildings is out-of-the-ordinary, and the most intriguing part of this dwelling's form. ∎

OPPOSITE Bluff top site above Mill Valley.

ABOVE View to San Francisco.

OPPOSITE
Covered walk alongside pool
connects the three pavillions.

ABOVE LEFT
Translucent fiberglass panels
protect the pool from blufftop
winds.

ABOVE RIGHT
Roofscape.

ABOVE LEFT
Bedroom with built-in
bookcase/closets surrounding
the bed.

ABOVE RIGHT
Wooden pavilion roof extends past
corner glass wall.

OPPOSITE
Living room with tall stone fireplace
and exposed beams at wood ceiling.

Moore/Lyndon/Turnbull/Whitaker
Condominium #9 Sea Ranch 1965

Charles Moore inhabited condominium #9 for nearly 30 years, from before construction was yet complete until his death; and it stands outside the sequence of houses he built when moving to take on the newest teaching job.

In the 1976 *Bay Area Houses*, Moore updates Dailey's formulation of the "Large-Small house," proposing the "small-great house." His place at Sea Ranch is an example, which he described in the February 1993 *Progressive Architecture*.

"For the past twenty-five-odd years, the Sea Ranch has been my Mother Earth; a place where I have gone, and continue to go, to have my energy and spirit rekindled. My condominium at the Sea Ranch has been a source of continuity and a constant in my life, which has been on the average anything but regular...

"When we were designing this cluster of condominiums, an important idea was to make the perimeter a defense against the sea and the elements, with the interior courts and rooms acting as protective shelters from the wind and weather. Every condominium contains a set of enclosures designed like large-scale 'furniture' that provides the living necessities — places for cooking, eating, and sleeping.

"Living with this condominium for such a long time has fine-tuned me to the rhythms of living in Northern California, and so has been a significant plus when designing homes for others desiring to live there." ■

OPPOSITE Designed as one large building, built from lumber cut nearby, the Sea Ranch condominiums slope down the bluff toward the Pacific Ocean.

ABOVE The drive leads to a parking courtyard. Condominium #9 forms the right corner of the building.

OPPOSITE
Charles Moore's colorful folk art, models, and textile collections contrast with the rough redwood exposed structure. The checkerboard "furniture" encloses the kitchen below and bath above.

ABOVE
Round wood posts, supporting the sleeping room above, enclose an intimate space by the wood burning stove. Beyond, wide window seats line the bay windows, overlooking the ocean.

ABOVE LEFT
Built in couch with four-poster
structure above on right, and
kitchen on left.

ABOVE RIGHT
Studio wing. Glass doors open to
sheltered entry courtyard on left.

OPPOSITE
View down from the third level
sleeping loft.

William Wurster Baer House & Studio Big Sur 1965

This is among Wurster's last houses, designed for the architectural and landscape photographer Morley Baer and his family. Like Baer's best known images, the dwelling is rendered in tones of black and white and warm grey. Interior floors are ebonized hardwood; walls and ceiling are painted a milky hue. The massive exterior walls are golden granite, quarried a few canyons away.

Ansel Adams, Baer's friend and neighbor, is said to have suggested the design of the great window, facing northwards up the Big Sur coast; its twelve sections of glass mirror the layout of a photographer's proof sheet. The proportions of the small windows are said to match those of an individual negative.

Most arresting is the house's extreme simplicity, an effect achieved without recourse to the now familiar deprivations of minimalism. Integral to this is the place's scale, which, unlike Wurster's earliest work, is relentlessly big.

Additions by Charles Moore and Roger Larson are smaller scale and less emphatic. ∎

OPPOSITE House and site from the south.

ABOVE House from Route 1.

OPPOSITE
The living room was frequently used as a gallery for exhibiting work by Baer and others. The large "contact sheet" window, overscaled fireplace washed by concealed skylights, and white walls and ceiling, form a setting especially congenial to black and white photographs.

ABOVE LEFT
House from below with archetypal Wurster oversized window.

ABOVE RIGHT
Stone walls and herringbone brick floor at the large kitchen.

ABOVE LEFT
Enclosed swimming pool.

ABOVE RIGHT
Glazed passageway to addition.

OPPOSITE
Redwood board addition.

John Davis **Barbour House** Kentfield 1967

While several well-known architects were early associated with Frank Lloyd Wright, none was more talented and accomplished, or less restrained, than Bruce Goff, whose unorthodox, freestyle buildings are a glory of American outsider architecture. In the mid-1940s, for just a year, Goff practiced in Berkeley, before making his way to the University of Oklahoma, where John Davis was his student.

This long, narrow, wood-sheathed dwelling, topped by a hovering, low-pitched roof, is more than a little reminiscent of Wright's early twentieth-century Prairie Houses. While the interior layout follows suit, it is also the setting for an effect that, in its flamboyant extravagance, must be called Goff-ian. The effect? — the long side of this long house simply rolls away. What was inside is, now, outside; what was a house is, now, a porch. What's more, the house now appears structurally unsupported, held aloft by unseen forces. (The secret is an ingenious truss.)

The Barbours, on the other hand, think of their house as a barn, and they're right. Their

only complaint is the occasional redwood splinter.

An engineer's miscalculation led to an unsightly retaining wall, and the need for a landscape architect to patch things up. "Who's the best?" asked Nancy Barbour. John Davis replied "Tommy Church, but he won't be interested." Church, Wurster's long-time collaborator, was soon on his way, enticed by Nancy's

husky voice. Over a good bottle of wine, the celebrated landscape architect described a handsome fix, sketched up on the spot. His fee? $100.

It makes me yearn for the 60s. ■

OPPOSITE Entry bridge leads beneath dramatically cantilevered roof.

ABOVE View from entry bridge to garden.

ABOVE LEFT
View from foyer to living areas
below and bedroom gallery above.

ABOVE MIDDLE
View from garden toward large,
cast-in-place concrete fireplace.

ABOVE RIGHT
View toward foyer and entry bridge
with tall glass doors open.

OPPOSITE
Living room adjacent to garden.

ABOVE LEFT
Long, narrow deck projects into
adjacent garden.

ABOVE RIGHT
Bedroom.

OPPOSITE
Kitchen and dining area from living
room.

David Ireland Ireland House San Francisco 1979

This Mission District Victorian house, builder-built in 1886, is colored a uniform dark grey, and is a bit shabby, the paint peeling at its edges. A fading sign, reverse-painted on the glass of the double-hung window adjacent to the front door, reads "ACCORDIONS". Up close, it is not clear that anyone lives here.

The impression is dispelled only slightly by the place's interior, which is lightly and eccentrically inhabited. There are the chairs on the walls, for example, and the pieces of concrete on the floor. The rooms are unusually shiny: the old, cracked plaster walls and ceilings and worn wood floors glisten beneath layers of varnish.

The feeling is of something like a haunted house.

The dwelling's animating spirit is artist David Ireland. Interviewed in connection with a recent retrospective at the Oakland Museum, he said, "Ideally my work has a visual presence that makes it seem like part of a usual, everyday situation. I like the feeling that nothing's been designed, that you can't tell where the art stops and starts."

Grey Brechin suggests that residing in a Maybeck house is like living in a Monet. Life at Ireland House, on the other hand, seems more like inhabiting a Duchamp. ∎

OPPOSITE Entrance hall.

ABOVE Outside, this Victorian dwelling appears simple, unaltered, and slighlty down at the heels — like houses in Edward Hopper paintings.

OPPOSITE
Layers of paint were stripped, and
the walls then coated with varnish.

ABOVE
Shapely and enigmatic objects
occupy table tops and vitrines.
Tall bay windows have their inner
workings exposed, their trim
removed and never returned.

ABOVE LEFT
Doorway to dining room.

ABOVE MIDDLE
Bedroom.

ABOVE RIGHT
Stair.

OPPOSITE
Dining room.

Robert A. M. Stern
Berggruen House San Francisco 1985

If the Bay Region style were a religion, this Russian Hill house would be sited on hallowed ground. There's a wonderful, early Julia Morgan house in the back yard; Willis Polk's place is around the corner; and houses by Coxhead and apartments by Esherick are just down the street. This dwelling is a substantial addition to and remodeling of one built in several stages beginning in the mid-nineteenth century, including an early iteration designed by Willis Polk.

The place's exterior, like that of much early Bay Region work, is eclectic, employing architectural elements in a variety of styles, especially classical. These are rendered in dark painted wood, set in and atop broad wood-shingled walls.

Inside, the place is an elegant, sympathetic, not-too-formal setting for art dealers Gretchen and John Berggruen's splendid collection.

At the lowest floor, not quite underground, conserved like an ancient artifact, is one room of the original Polk-designed cottage. ■

OPPOSITE Brown shingle front with black painted wood trim and classical detail.

ABOVE LEFT View from foyer back down long entry stair.

ABOVE MIDDLE Palladian opening at street front repeats in plaster along the stair.

ABOVE RIGHT The upper floor is set back, creating extensive terraces with panoramic views of San Francisco.

OPPOSITE
Lacewood-paneled stair walls rise
two stories to a skylit top.

ABOVE LEFT
Stairway from foyer to main living
floor.

ABOVE RIGHT
Library, with window to stair hall.

ABOVE LEFT
Built-in casework in bathroom is
designed to resemble furniture.

ABOVE RIGHT
Large painting fills a classical niche
in bedroom.

OPPOSITE
Living room with tall, vaulted ceiling
and light plaster walls is designed to
display large works of art.

Ace Architects Darrell Place San Francisco 1989

From *Ten Houses: Ace Architects* —

"If in the nineteenth-century eclecticism was often the default approach to architectural design, for much of the twentieth century it was something of a dirty word. Modernist Mumford's interest in the Bay Region style did not, of course, extend to its eclecticism.

"This building, on the other hand, housing two apartments on the eastern slope of Telegraph Hill, set among some of the oldest houses in San Francisco, is fully eclectic. While employing the Bay Region style's attitude toward materials, allusion, and the out-of-doors, it also reconstitutes some of its memorable forms.

"The narrow site faces a much narrower pedestrian lane and is inaccessible to vehicles. Toward this lane, the building appears a fanciful reconstruction of a place made up over time, assembled of pieces from the history of the Bay Region style, beginning in the late nineteenth century. Toward San Francisco Bay, the architecture rises like the cities of Troy — a newer story built atop an older story, topped by still another layer.

"This approach includes the building's interior, where the lower apartment is gotten up in the early Bay Region's classicizing dress, while the upper apartment sports its International Style and, later, vernacular, and aedicular refinements." ∎

OPPOSITE View from interior balcony, across rooftops, toward San Francisco Bay.

ABOVE Rear view of house. Seahorse railing is of painted steel plate, cut with a laser-guided torch.

OPPOSITE
Painted plaster figures of Sculpture and Architecture flank stairs at the foyer.

ABOVE
Vertical grain redwood-plywood walls provide a setting for stained plywood table and chairs.

ABOVE LEFT
Steel and glass doors lead from
the terrace into marble and slate
floored bedroom.

ABOVE RIGHT
Modeled on a vaulted undercroft,
the bedroom is at the building's
lowest floor, partly below grade.
"Skylight" is from glass bricks set
into the floor of the living room
above.

OPPOSITE
Yellow-hued Architecture Room
is a ten-foot cube. Ceiling mural
pictures the several periods of the
Bay Region style.

Mark Bulwinkle **Bulwinkleland** Oakland 1986

In 1924, on the site where his own house had burned a year earlier, Maybeck built a studio for himself the walls of which were made of Bubblestone, a concrete material a friend of his had cooked up. Burlap bags, first dipped in Bubblestone, were strung on wires across wood framing, and the effect was picturesque.

Fifty years later, in the same spirit, Mark Bulwinkle decorated his unremarkable old house in a somewhat tony North Oakland neighborhood, with a forest of rusted steel plate, torch cut into shapes of fantastical people and animals. By the time he left for Bulwinkleland, it was difficult to see the house for its decoration. Because it was located on Manila Avenue, and the third Ali-Frazier fight was not yet forgotten, some called that house the "Thrilla in Manila."

By comparison, Bulwinkleland, in rough-and-ready West Oakland, is a project at an almost civic scale, including the artist's home, shop, construction yard, and a variety of structures containing special collections, stretching across the middle of two city blocks. ∎

OPPOSITE Decorated, corrugated steel Quonset hut houses work and living spaces.

ABOVE Studio.

OPPOSITE
Colorful Bulwinkle creatures in
several materials hang from
exposed metal ribs and cavort
along tables set on unfinished
plywood floor.

ABOVE LEFT
Antique printing equipment.

ABOVE MIDDLE
Bedroom.

ABOVE RIGHT
Kitchen.

ABOVE LEFT
Trailer interior.

ABOVE RIGHT
Collections of metal objects,
Bulwinkle's own work, and objects
by other artists are arranged along
a route interspersed with small
special purpose trailers.

OPPOSITE
Sculpture fabrication yard.

Jeremy Kotas Torre San Gimigniano San Francisco 1990

Laidley Avenue in San Francisco's Diamond Heights is lined with several highly eccentric houses designed by Jeremy Kotas and his collaborators in the 1980s and early 1990s.

This house, whose Italo-phile owners Bill Gregory and Dick Ingraham named it after the medieval Italian town famous for competitive tower building, is called by others, affectionately, Owl House, owing to the facade's quizzically arched "eyebrows."

Kotas, a Coxhead expert, working with Skip Shaffer at Acme Romance Architects, devised the front as a loose, eclectic, homage to the early- and middle-Bay Region style. Dark painted wood decorative elements are set into a tall wood-shingled wall. An impossibly large window, set up to be double hung, is outlined with big-scale picture frame molding, a favorite device of Gardner Dailey.

Kotas is also an alumnus of Frank Gehry's studio, which is little surprise once you're inside. A great whorl of a stair rises up through the center of the house. Along this corkscrew route, bits and pieces of the place swirl into and out of focus, as with the cyclone in the Wizard of Oz. The vaguely elliptical plan of the stair recalls Baroque Rome, whose most notoriously talented architect, Francesco Borromini, had he been working in San Francisco in the late twentieth century, for clients who love Italy, might have designed a house like this one. ■

OPPOSITE Owl-like eyebrows top an enormous "double-hung" window at the tall, narrow shingle facade.

ABOVE Richly colored entry foyer leads to light-filled stairway.

OPPOSITE
Elliptical stair whirls into the
multi-level living space. Corrugated
metal wall reflects light from
irregulary placed skylights set
above ceiling framing.

ABOVE LEFT
Kitchen with red lacquer
casework.

ABOVE MIDDLE
View along bridge toward
over-sized front window.

ABOVE RIGHT
Steel treads cantilever from the
sloping wall to form an unnerving
staircase.

ABOVE
Corrugated metal closets roll
around the bedroom.

OPPOSITE
The roof framing runs through
a group of three cattywompus
skylights.

William Turnbull and Mary Griffin

Teviot Springs Vineyard Calistoga 1991

The architects write that their vineyard house, built largely with their own hands, is inspired by Charles Keeler's famous equation of Hillside Architecture and Landscape Gardening. For once, it is impossible to disagree. Their description continues:

"The house, only ten feet wide, and its companion building, a wash house, flank two opposite ends of an eighty-foot-by-eighty-foot carpet of grass. A fieldstone wall at one side anchors this outdoor living room into the hillside, behind which rises a dark forested slope of evergreen trees. The other side of the lawn, defined by a stand of mature oak trees, opens out to the valley below. The tree canopy makes a shady summertime dining room with a wood chip-covered floor. A four posted tree house with a children's sleeping platform above and an outdoor bath below also sits nestled in this grove. On a hill high in the vineyard stands a gazebo, built as the owners' wedding chapel, which looks out over the landscape.

"The house is a simple, narrow gabled-roof building punctuated in the middle by a pass-through covered porch. In the summer with the sliding doors open, the

porch serves as a breezeway and dining room. In winter with the doors closed, the porch becomes a mud room and sun room. All year long it lends privacy to the two halves of the house it separates; bed and bath on one side and living spaces on the other.

"The house is knitted into the existing landscape in material as well as form. Except for the metal chimney, the house might as easily have been built in 1882 as 1992." ∎

OPPOSITE View of house from lawn, with breezeway open to vineyard beyond. Sliding glass doors rolled to the side match French doors at the living room.

ABOVE Breezeway is the dining room in warm weather.

OPPOSITE
Window seat with built-in
bookcases on either side fills the
bay at the end.

ABOVE LEFT
Elegantly assembled exposed fir
framing, walls, and casework at the
main living space.

ABOVE RIGHT
Fir walls and exposed framing carry
through to the bedroom.

ABOVE LEFT
Chapel overlooking the vineyard,
— a simple trellised redwood frame,
was constructed by Mary and Bill
for their marriage.

ABOVE RIGHT
Fruit trees and vegetable garden
in front of the wash house, with
lawn and house beyond.

OPPOSITE
Bay window in the ten-foot-wide
gable end, flanked by fruit trees.

Mark Mack **Stonewall** Berkeley 1996

Mark Mack came to the Bay Area from Austria, with a three year layover in architect Emilio Ambasz's New York office, in 1976; and he arrived with a flourish. Almost immediately, he initiated a popular architecture lecture series and founded *Archetype*, a sober, local architectural journal. In partnership and on his own he designed a series of starkly handsome houses, closely tied to their sites. By 1993, he had left for Los Angeles.

Designed after Mack decamped, this 1996 addition, including exterior stairs, a tower study, and other improvements, at first appears an uncharacteristic work. Though the stair employs his vivid geometries, Mack's work is just subtly distinguished from the original house.

This house, built in 1927, is itself an uncharacteristic work, designed by William Wurster in the year before his career-launching Gregory Farmhouse. In addition to this Mediterranean-style dwelling, Wurster in the same year designed houses gotten up French Regency and Spanish Colonial Revival. Success later narrowed the range of Wurster's eclectic appetites, but hardly made them less voracious. ∎

OPPOSITE The study addition pokes above the original roof, matching it closely in pitch, color, and texture. The Owner wished to recall Mediterranean, rooftop drying towers.

ABOVE LEFT View from the street.

ABOVE RIGHT Characteristic Wurster extra-wide front door opens onto foyer, on axis with view to San Francisco Bay.

ABOVE LEFT
Mark Bulwinkle-designed gate
memorializes owner's late dog.

ABOVE MIDDLE
Study addition with windows on all
sides is a miniature of living room.

ABOVE RIGHT
Double stair addition allows garden
access from main living level.

OPPOSITE
Living room with highly crafted
exposed wood frame ceiling.

Mickey Muennig Partington Point House Big Sur 1996

In the late 1970s, the flamboyant and idiosyncratic Oklahoma architect Bruce Goff arrived in Berkeley to lecture at the university. A genial-looking fellow, he wore a bright gingham shirt, bolo tie, and cowboy boots. The talk that evening, more like a series of stories told round a campfire, was unforgettable.

One of them went like this. Mr. Goff was standing in front of one of his strange-looking Oklahoma houses, when the woman from next door walked up. She asked about the dark, unusual material making up the walls. "That's coal," replied Goff. "But, Mr. Goff, can't coal catch fire?" she objected. "Yes, it can," Goff replied, asking "Is that your house?" "Yes it is," she replied. "What are the walls made of?" Goff queried. "Wood," the lady responded.

Mickey Muennig was Goff's student at the University of Oklahoma in Norman, and later worked in Goff's Bartlesville office. Following the success of his Post Ranch Resort in Big Sur, reporter Lucie Young profiled Muennig for the *New York Times*. She wrote: "… he recently built a new house … It is almost totally underground. It is easy to come

upon the house from the back and find yourself standing atop its sod roof. Mr. Muennig is considering making the skylights retractable, but worries that local wild pigs will come crashing into the living room."

Though Muennig isn't partial to western attire, he retains a considerable drawl, and must have spun some good stories for the lady from the *Times*. The acorn, they say, doesn't fall far from the oak.

This house, perched on a promontory overlooking the Pacific Ocean, is among the more sober in Muennig's oeuvre, more indebted to Goff's hero Frank Lloyd Wright, than the wild cowboy architect from Bartlesville. ∎

OPPOSITE Perched on a precipice high above the Pacific Ocean, the two-story glass pavilion houses the living and dining areas.

ABOVE Kitchen and master bedroom are in this low wing.

OPPOSITE & ABOVE LEFT
Living room with view to the
Pacific. Transparent deck fabricated
from steel plate, rod and perforated
mesh.

ABOVE MIDDLE
Kitchen.

ABOVE RIGHT
Large soaking tub on balcony
overlooking living room.

ABOVE LEFT
Master bedroom with horizontal
board pattern on concrete wall.

ABOVE RIGHT
Wide roof overhang of main
pavilion.

OPPOSITE
Master bath with view north along
the Big Sur coast.

Kuth/Raineri Ian/Stolz House San Francisco 1999

This small, up-to-the-minute house on the northern slope of Nob Hill extends the Bay Region style's history of dwellings made as highly crafted cabinets. The front of this place is even finished in mahogany — a surprisingly reasonable, if luxe, choice, as redwood, the Bay Area's characteristic building material for almost two centuries, is no longer of dependable quality.

With the front and garage doors neatly camouflaged, the front of the building, like certain early Bay Region-style houses, has a strangely indeterminate scale. This facade, say the architects, is an abstraction of the house and its setting. Perhaps so.

Inside, the place hews closely to Dailey's fifty-year-old formulation of the "Large-Small House." One large room contains living and dining, while stairs and service areas are minimized. This is done so suavely and with such sophistication, that it might be called Dailey-esque.

Upstairs, with panels swung away, and portions of the exterior wall made to vanish, the effect is of an elegant sleeping porch. ∎

OPPOSITE Street facade of clear sealed mahogany ledges and panels.

ABOVE At foyer, black steel stairs lead to main living space.

OPPOSITE
View toward living room with
"floating" ceiling over steel faced
fireplace.

ABOVE LEFT
View through living room to dining
area beyond

ABOVE RIGHT
Stone dining room floor appears
suspended above wood floor of
living room.

ABOVE LEFT
Tub with pivoting wall open.

ABOVE RIGHT
Roof-deck view toward Golden
Gate Bridge.

OPPOSITE
Bedroom wall slides away for open
air sleeping; while bathroom wall
behind bed pivots out of the way.

Fernau & Hartman **West Marin House** Marin County 2000

The impression is of an idiosyncratic miniature village assembled, perhaps, by an eccentric country builder who, over the years, was unable to suppress his serial and enthusiastic plans for improving the place.

Roofs fly up unexpectedly, walls roll away, bays jut, metal sunscreens hang over different windows in different ways. Walls are horizontally-sided, except when they're vertically-sided, or finished in stucco, or concrete. With all this, the house seems absolutely at home on its site, a clearing set amongst oak trees.

David Gebhard cites Wurster's use of the "visual language of the rural vernacular." With Wurster, the vernacular is a source for making highly-idealized, simple-appearing, livable dwellings. This house's use of the vernacular, on the other hand, focuses on what Charles Moore called its "unguarded response" — a kind of circumstantial problem-solving whose architectural credo is — "Who cares what it looks like." Here, this path leads to a house as livable as any of

Wurster's, while less idealized, and hardly simple.

This house's embrace of the vernacular runs just so far, though. Unlike the gimcrack construction of its sources, this house is very carefully, even precisely, wrought; and the interior is hardly the pokey, low-ceilinged box of an old rural farmhouse. ∎

OPPOSITE Diminuitive tower marks entry. Light-colored plaster walls are highly insulating straw bale construction.

ABOVE A small house made of diminuitive pieces, set along the edge of a grassy clearing edged by Oak trees.

OPPOSITE
Living room with rolling glass
garage doors, concrete floor, and
fireplace. Wheeled couch converts
to bed that rolls outside.

ABOVE LEFT
Living room exterior.

ABOVE RIGHT
Concrete pizza oven with steel
canopy at a corner of the central
courtyard.

ABOVE LEFT
View down from study along
bookcase wall.

ABOVE MIDDLE
Nook in straw bale wall, with wood
burning stove.

ABOVE RIGHT
Breakfast room under complex
exposed roof framing.

OPPOSITE
View to dining and sitting room
from kitchen. Highly crafted
casework and roof framing.

Howard Backen Napa Valley House Napa 2001

The left-leaning Berkeley radio station KPFA used to conclude its news broadcasts with a call to arms — "Don't like the news? Go make some of your own!" Perhaps the show still ends this way.

The eighteenth century, with the rise of the Picturesque, heard a related exhortation — "Don't like the landscape? Go make one of your own!"

Romantic era landscape gardeners arranged and re-arranged hills and forests, rivers and herds of cattle, and, importantly, buildings to make places sufficiently picturesque. In part, the idea was to make nature appear more, well, natural. The Picturesque has been an animating idea of the Bay Region style from its beginnings, applied not just to landscape, but to houses and the way they fit the variety of their settings, from rural to urban.

With this house, in the shadow of Napa Valley's Stag's Leap Palisades, it's as though an elegant houseboat had floated up to the lake's edge, then lingered too long, allowing nearby vegetation time to grow and ensnare it. Gentle and handsome, the place is radically picturesque — constructed alongside a man-made lake, within an invented topography of new planting extending from the adjacent landscape across its rooftops. The effect is of nature appearing, well, more natural. ∎

OPPOSITE Landscape sweeps onto the roof of the house at the edge of the pond.

ABOVE Steps lead toward entry through garden.

OPPOSITE
Garden.

ABOVE LEFT
Living room with criss-cross
hemlock and plaster ceiling, stone
fireplace, and stone base at walls.

ABOVE RIGHT
Living room with wall open to pond.

OPPOSITE
Boatlike, the house cantilevers over the pond. Boat at far left is guest room.

ABOVE LEFT
Wide pocket doors open the house to the pond.

ABOVE RIGHT
Plan of the house follows the water's edge.

ABOVE LEFT
Bedroom.

ABOVE MIDDLE
Bath.

ABOVE RIGHT
Soaking tub shaped like a small
boat.

OPPOSITE
View from bedroom toward pond
and mountain beyond.

Artists and Architects
The Orchard for Artists / Villa Montalvo Saratoga 2004

Throughout its history, signal Bay Region-style houses have been designed both by architects and artists for themselves, and by architects for artists. Examples included here are Willis Polk's house for the painter Mrs. Virgil Williams; poet Robinson Jeffers' Tor House, and the Owings' Wild Bird; Charles Moore's and William Turnbull's houses; Wurster's house for photographer Morley Baer; and David Ireland's and Mark Bulwinkle's dwellings. Bay Area real estate prices have long since climbed beyond the stratosphere, and this type of Bay Region-style house jeopardized.

Villa Montalvo, an arts organization initiated by the nineteenth-century San Francisco banker and politician James Phelan, and located on his 175-acre estate, has revived the idea of the architect designed artist's home in a very big way.

Five architects — including three from San Francisco and one who left — worked with artists and writers — including David Ireland and the Bay Area environmental artist Doug Hollis — to devise ten live/work studios for visiting artists.

The houses are invigorating, simple, and small-scale; fully

contemporary, yet picturesque and intimately tied to the abandoned orchard which is their site.

Are these Bay Region-style houses? When, almost fifty years ago, Wild Bird was just complete atop its rocky Big Sur promontory, there was alarm over its strident, then naked form. With the softenings of time, and its inundation by the

landscape, the place has become iconic, not just of the Bay Region style, but of a way of living along the Northern California coast. ∎

OPPOSITE One of Jim Jennings' Visual Artists and Writers Cottages on the hillside.

ABOVE Environmental artist Herb Parker's sod temple "Caracol" on the lawn of the Italianate Villa Montalvo.

Dan Solomon

Twin Composers Cottages by
Architect Dan Solomon with
Composer Patrick Gleeson and
visual artist Nellie Solomon.

ABOVE LEFT
Gently curving wooden trellises
cover porches along both cottage
fronts.

ABOVE RIGHT
The pair of houses are set into
the hill at the rear, a type of
construction designed to control
acoustics.

Jim Jennings

Architect Jim Jennings collaborated
with sculptor Richard Serra and
poet Czeslaw Milosc on two Visual
Artists and Writers Cottages.

ABOVE LEFT
The upper, more severe, Jennings'
cottage seen from the cottage
below.

ABOVE RIGHT
The building on the left is a single
room with transparent walls, which,
at night, glow like a lantern.

Hodgetts and Fung

Architects Hodgetts and Fung collaborated with playwright Lee Breuer on two Writers Cottages.

ABOVE LEFT
The upper "introverted" cottage.

ABOVE RIGHT
Rooftops of the colorful lower "extroverted" cottage, seen from connecting bridge. Jennings and Santos buildings in background.

Adele Santos

Architect Adele Santos worked with artist Doug Hollis on two Visual Artists Cottages.

OPPOSITE ABOVE LEFT
Roof curves up at living area and curves down at workspace area.

Mark Mack

Architect Mark Mack collaborated with conceptual artist David Ireland's on Visual Artists cottages.

ABOVE RIGHT The two cottages face one another across a common yard.

Sod Temple

PAGE 204
The "Caracol," with grass covered columns, spirals around into a rammed earth chamber. From above, an oculus illumines an earthen bench.

Twig Chapel

PAGE 205
"A Capella," a twig baroque chapel by artist Patrick Dougherty, is sited on the Villa lawn, forming, with the nearby "Caracol," a remarkable, though sadly temporary, pair of picturesque garden follies.

Enthusiasms
and Appreciations

Having set our sights on a house we thought promising for this book, it was left to contact the place's inhabitants, and sound them out. This took several forms. Best, of course, was when we were already acquainted; and second best when we knew someone in common. Further down the food chain was a carefully composed form letter and/or the telephone and subsequent cold call. When even these methods failed, and desperation set in, we resorted to walking the streets, ringing doorbells, the architectural equivalents of Jehovah's Witnesses.

One of those doorbells belonged to a very high example of a very picturesque, perhaps French-styled, storybook house from the 1920s. I felt certain that those living there, who I imagined as picturesque, perhaps French-styled elves, would embrace the project. The doorbell rang and the sweet voice of a little girl invited us into the forecourt, where we were met by two teenage boys. They looked at each other skeptically when we asked to speak with their parents, but were agreeable, and retreated inside to arrange the meeting. At the edge of the court, the top half of a Dutch door swung open, and a small, yes elfin, figure beckoned.

In the course of our pitch we realized, surprisingly slowly, that this was no elf, but a computer industry titan (actually a titan among titans). Though famous for, among many things, not suffering fools gladly, he heard us out, before, almost politely, declining.

Lewis Mumford wrote in 1949 of Bay Region architects' "impulse to bury their lights under a bushel, so foreign to our usual American tendency to over- expose, over-publicize, over-claim." Much of this has made its way, as well, to those living in Bay Region-style houses, at least those we visited, none of whom seemed really eager to be included here. Still, the great majority decided to proceed, and bear the strangers on their doorsteps, and in their living rooms.

In some instances, this occurred as much from duty as graciousness. One woman, living with her family in a not spacious set of rooms set on several levels of an early Bay Region-style landmark, has given up one of her diminutive floors, for essentially curatorial purposes. Apparently, her neighbors and others, like us, are constantly asking to see the house.

Generally, reticence gave way not to politeness, but to an almost startling enthusiasm for dwelling. These people love to live in their houses. This was especially vivid in the tours they led, which, though often covering very little physical territory, were expansive discussions, touching not only on architecture and history; but on politics, economics, and carpentry; personality, celebrity, and fashion; family background, neighbors, and, this being California, the real estate market. These were often long tours for little houses, though never long-winded. Time after time, these were descriptions of entire domestic universes, not just related to Bay Region-style houses, but entirely caught up and contained within them.

Part of what makes even the oldest Bay Region-style houses invigorating, I think, is that they continue to be inhabited; and so remain part of the Bay Area's collective domestic life. This is unlike historic houses elsewhere, which are too often embalmed as house museums. These sorts of relics are houses the same way a stuffed lion is a predatory jungle cat.

Because they remain in private hands, though, Bay Region-style houses face other risks. While earthquake and fire, development and carelessness have exacted a considerable toll on the early work of Maybeck, Polk, Coxhead, Morgan, and many others, those houses which survive now seem largely secure.

By contrast, important houses from the 1930s through to the 1960s, by Wurster, Gardner Dailey, and others are regularly demolished or remodeled out of existence. Many of these, ample in their time, are now too small for the lavishly sized, exorbitantly priced real estate on which they are sited. Ironically, it is now easier to locate an intact house by Maybeck, many of whose houses were incinerated in the disastrous 1923 Berkeley fire, than a characteristic house by the prolific Wurster. That so many mid-century Bay Region houses survive is due, almost solely, to their owners' enduring enthusiasms for them.

In a similar way, this project relied on many other people's generous enthusiasms for the entire, ongoing phenomenon of Bay Region-style houses.

Lucia Howard, my partner in every large endeavor, early understood and helped shape this project's essential elements; and worked through the vast number of bogglingly complex arrangements.

Without Bay Region-style houses to write about and photograph, this wouldn't be much of a book. Many thanks to all those who generously allowed us into their houses, including Don and Nancy Barbour, Joy Bartlett, Gretchen and John Berggruen, Mark Bulwinkle, Cass and Marlene Candell, Ron and Denise Cox, Carol Fisch, Faega and Wallace Friedman, Bill Gregory and Richard Ingraham, Mary Griffiin, Adriane Iann and Christian Stolz, David Ireland, Ray Lifchez, David and Sheila Littlejohn, Don McLeod, Salvador Mendoza, Mickey Muennig, Susan and Paul Opsvig, Robert Pence, Katy Rees at Villa Montalvo, Bill Roberts, Carol Ann and Nielsen Rogers, Jane Roos LeRoux, Susan Schindler, and Alex Vardamis at the Robinson Jeffers Tor House Foundation.

Many of the architects whose houses are pictured here also abetted our work, including: Anni Arkin, Howard Backen, Mary Griffin, Laura Hartman, Jeremy Kotas, Byron Kuth, Donlyn Lyndon, Robert Stern, Claude Stoller, and Bruce Tomb. Thanks, also, to Alice Carey, Peter Dodge, Craig Hudson, and Waverly Lowell.

We received expert and candid advice from several leading Bay Area architectural historians, especially Betty Marvin, as well as Anthony Bruce, Dan Gregory, and Alan Hess.

Many thanks to the patient Zand Gee, who has designed yet another beautiful book.

At Rizzoli International Publications, we are especially grateful to our editor David Morton, who supported the project; and to Douglas Curran, who saw it through.

In the 1949 *Domestic Architecture of the San Francisco Bay Region*, William Wurster complained of photography — "these wonderful houses (of Coxhead, Polk, Howard, Maybeck, and others) were enjoyed and exclaimed over, but they defy photography. And they should, for you can seldom take a picture of space, as it can only show surface at the end of space." I wonder if this observation doesn't have in mind images of Wurster's work, as well. His more Internationally Styled house interiors of the 1930s and 40s, compelling in person, if they don't "defy photography," are famously resistant. Historically, the Bay Area has been beyond fortunate in its wealth of architectural photographers, many of whom were aligned with the medium's great California artists, including Edward Weston and Ansel Adams. This book includes images by Roger Sturtevant and Morley Baer, two of the most important northern California photographers, whose work, as much as anyone's, fostered the spread of interest in Bay Region-style houses. We are grateful to the College of Environmental Design Archives for use of the Sturtevant images; and to Joshua Baer, for use of his father's photographs.

Finally, I want to thank John Beach, by way of remembering him and his famous enthusiasm for Bay Region-style houses, especially those which, like John, were off-beat, fun, and thoroughly eccentric. ∎